Does Anyone Care How I Feel?

Does Anyone Care How I Feel?

MILDRED TENGBOM

BETHANY HOUSE PUBLISHERS

MINNEAPOLIS, MINNESOTA 55438

A Division of Bethany Fellowship, Inc.

All Scripture references are taken from the *Revised Standard Version* of the Bible, unless otherwise noted.

Photos by: Dick Easterday and Fred Renich

Published by Bethany Fellowship, Inc.
6820 Auto Club Road, Minneapolis, Minnesota 55438

Printed in the United States of America

Library of Congress Cataloging in Publication Data

Tengbom, Mildred.
    Does anyone care how I feel?

    Summary: Includes fifty-two short devotionals about commonly experienced situations with emphasis upon family members sharing their feelings about the situations.
    1. Children—Prayer-books and devotions—English. [1. Prayer books and devotions] I. Title.
BV4870.T4   242   81-3808
ISBN 0-87123-142-5   AACR2

The Author

MILDRED TENGBOM was born in Minnesota, and at an early age developed a passion for reading and writing. At age 15 Christ became real to her, and she eventually went to the borders of Nepal as a missionary. After her marriage to Dr. Tengbom, she served again as a missionary—this time in East Africa. The Tengboms have two sons and two daughters, all followers of Christ. Mrs. Tengbom has written several books. Her work has been published in over fifty secular and religious periodicals.

Books by Mildred Tengbom

Is Your God Big Enough?
The Bonus Years
Table Prayers
Fill My Cup, Lord
No Greater Love: The Story of Clara Louise Maass
A Life to Cherish
Especially for Mother
Sometimes I Hurt
Bible Readings for Families
Help for Bereaved Parents

Table of Contents

A Word to Parents*

The importance of family members sharing how they feel about things in a constructive and helpful way hit me when we were airborne in a plane in Africa. This is what happened.

Our family spent eight and one-half years on the lower slopes of Kilimanjaro, East Africa, while our children were growing up. As each began to smile with the winsome smile of a toothless six-year-old, we had to put our young son or daughter on a bus to be sent to a boarding school 300 miles away. The children would be gone for three months, return home for a month, then go again for three months, etc. Being separated from them in this way was a heart-crushing experience, but we tried to "bear up" and be brave, especially when we waved good-bye to them as they left on the bus.

Finally the time came when our entire family returned to the United States. That morning a cluster of African friends rode the bus or walked to the airport to see us off. At the airport the group surrounded our family, and then sang and sang and finally prayed, committing us to God's care. The pilot stood watching the little drama with interest.

After we were airborne, our pilot abandoned the usual route and instead flew directly over the saddle between the two peaks, Mawenzi and Kibo. Then he dipped the wings of our plane as though in farewell to the mountain.

I had become very attached to the mountain which had sheltered our family on her bosom for so many years. As the wings of our plane dipped in farewell, the deeps within me suddenly burst through my carefully guarded reserve, and I began to sob. Our eight-year-old Janet, who was sitting a few seats in front of me,

---

*Please don't attempt to use this book without reading this introduction.

heard me and walked back. Standing in the aisle surveying me, she put her hands on her hips and said, "Serves you right!"

"What do you mean?" I stammered.

"Serves you right," she repeated. "Now you know how your little kids felt every time you sent them off to school!"

Startled, I awoke to the realization that by not telling my children how much it hurt me to have to send them away to school, I had given the impression that I didn't care much at all. What they interpreted as my indifference only added to their hurt.

That day, while I flew across the domed skies of East Africa, I resolved to begin to express freely to my family how I *felt* about different things.

As good parents we care for the physical, intellectual, social and spiritual needs of our children. But how much attention do we give to developing good *emotional* health? Because of my concern, I have designed this little book to help all members of the family:

1. Understand their own feelings in different situations.
2. Learn to communicate their feelings to each other.
3. Grow in understanding of God, themselves, and others.

I have tried to bear in mind seven keys to good emotional health:

1. The assurance of being loved.
2. Preparedness for situations and troubles that will come eventually.
3. The ability to express my feelings—especially negative feelings—and knowing how to vent them in acceptable ways.
4. Willingness to admit I am sometimes bad and do wrong things.
5. Freedom to speak and act as I really am and feel, and not having to pretend.
6. Feeling good about myself and being free to recognize and value my strengths and abilities.
7. Assurance that God understands me. Although He is far above me, and I can never, in this life, be perfect in every way as He is perfect, He loves me and can enable me to be all that I'm meant to be right now.

There are fifty-two devotionals in the book. You may choose to set aside one particular night each week and use this book as a springboard for "family sharing." Or you may choose to turn to the book as situations arise when feelings need to be uncovered and discussed. The more familiar you as parents are with the contents of the book, the more useful it will be to you.

Create a "ritual" by which you can introduce the use of the book on certain nights. For example, you could design a mobile of hearts with open doors, and hang this mobile from the light fixture over your table on nights you will be using the book. Or you could use the book as a centerpiece. Or you could light a candle of a certain color and place it in the center of the table. This would signal to the children that the evening holds a special time of "family sharing."

I have designed the book so that *children* read the portions and ask the questions for discussion. This is important.

It is absolutely necessary that you allow sufficient time for relaxed, unhurried discussion. Anything you can do to create a "mood" will help. In the winter you might want to gather in front of the fireplace. In the summer you may have a spot in the backyard or a nearby park which you enjoy. Some of the happiest sharing times our family had took place when all six of us fit ourselves together on top of the big bed in our bedroom. (Arranging ourselves on the bed was always prefaced with much hilarity.) Rainy days or snowy, windy days also help, in their own special way, to create an atmosphere of coziness inside the house. Be sensitive to these opportunities.

I can't stress enough the importance of you as parents being honest and open with your children about how you feel. The degree to which family members are able to open up to each other will determine largely the benefit you gain from using this book.

Remember, however, that "sharing time" is *not* a time to scold or reprimand, or to remind each other of past failings and mistakes. It is not a time to "tell off" or "get even." Instead it should be a time of strongly supporting one another, a time of developing understanding and love for each other. Hurts and negative feelings should be lovingly guided to forgiveness and healing.

In the back of the book I have included some blank pages

where you may record your own "share and tell" stories.

I have not specifically instructed that at the close of every session you as a family pray together. I assume you will naturally want to do this. When we pray, we open our hearts to a God who understands us far better than we shall ever understand ourselves. He also understands us better than anyone else ever can. He can give healing and peace in full measure. Therefore, we turn constantly, expectantly, and joyfully to Him.

Memorizing the Bible verses referred to at the close of each section also would enrich the entire family.

Much of the book actually was "written" by children, in that they opened up their hearts to me and told me how they felt in different situations. I am indebted to them and say thank you to them for the honor of entrusting me with some of the secret thoughts of their hearts.

I want to thank also my friend, Linda Gunn, mother of three, teacher, and Director of Christian Education, who critiqued this book and offered many helpful suggestions.

1

Being Alone and Feeling Good

I like my tree house, Jesus.
It's so far above the rest of the world.
The wind blows softly through the leaves,
  and I feel all alone and good.
I like having a special place like this for getting away.
Whenever I feel all mixed up about something,
  I disappear up here.
Somehow it's easier to sort things out
  all alone
  in my special place.
Only I wish Mom would leave me alone.
Doesn't she understand that sometimes kids
  don't want to be asked all kinds of questions?

Let's Talk

1. All of us need times to be alone. Where do you like to go to be alone?

2. Why is it nice to be alone?

3. What do you do when you are alone?

4. How do you feel when you're alone?

5. Jesus also liked to spend some time alone. Sometimes He went up to the mountains. When He was alone He spent some of His time talking to God.

  a. Have you ever talked to God when you were alone?

  b. What did you tell Him?

  c. How does it feel to be all alone together—just Jesus and you?

6. Where does Mother go to be alone?

7. Where does Dad go to be alone?

8. Ask Mom and Dad how they feel at the end of a very busy day when they haven't had any time just for themselves.

9. Ask your parents how they feel when they come home from work at night.

10. Some mothers say the only place they can go to be alone is in the bathroom, and even there the kids will stand outside and pound on the door. What can your family do to help Mom and Dad have some time of their own?

Verses to Remember:

"Be still, and know that I am God" (Ps. 46:10).

"In quietness and in trust shall be your strength" (Isa. 30:15).

2

My Team Lost Again

Lord, the Twins lost again last night.
They were so close to winning the pennant.
I wanted them to win.
I felt so bad I crawled into the closet.
I felt like sitting there in the dark forever.
This morning I saw the flowers in church, Lord,
    and thought,
       they're in memory of the Twins who lost last night.
It's tough when the team you're rooting for loses.
Oh, well, I guess there'll always be another season, won't there?

Let's Talk

1. What team do you cheer for?
    a. Are they winning or losing?
    b. How do you feel when they win?
    c. How do you feel when they lose?
2. Ask Mother and Dad to share examples of when they succeeded at something and when they failed. Ask them how they felt when they won and when they lost.
3. All of us like to win, but many times in life we'll lose. When we don't succeed right away, we have to think about the power of *persistence*. Persistence means to keep on trying.
    a. Abraham Lincoln didn't become president right away.
    Listen to his record:
    Lost job—1832.
    Defeated for Illinois legislature—1832.
    Failed in business—1833.
    Elected to state legislature—1834.

Sweetheart died—1835.

Nervous breakdown—1836.

Defeated for speaker—1838.

Defeated for nomination for congress—1843.

Elected to congress—1846.

Lost renomination—1848.

Rejected for federal land officer appointment—1849.

Defeated for senate—1854.

Defeated for nomination for vice-president—1856.

Again defeated for senate—1858.

Elected president—1860.

b. When Althea Gibson won a tennis championship at Wimbledon, she said her coach had helped her win. Ms. Gibson said, "My coach used to say to me, 'Faith is *believing* something steadily. Persistence is *doing* something steadily in spite of opposition and discouragement."

4. What are some goals you would like to reach but haven't been able to yet?

5. What has prevented you from reaching some of your goals?

6. Can Mother and Dad tell about some of their goals which took persistence for them to obtain?

A Verse to Remember:

"And let us not grow weary in well-doing, for in due season we shall reap, if we do not lose heart" (Gal. 6:9).

3

My Friend Is Sick

My friend is sick, Lord, and I wish
   there were something I could do for him.
Maybe I could bring him my favorite book.
Do you think that would make him happy?

Let's Talk

1. Tell about a time when you were sick and had to stay in bed.
   a. How did you feel?
   b. What helped you feel better?
2. Jesus was always interested in helping the sick. Who were some people whom He made well? (Luke 4:38-39; Luke 5:12-15; Luke 6:6-11).
3. Proverbs 17:22 tells us about some good medicine we can bring to our friends when they are sick. Look up the verse to see what that medicine is.
4. Do you know someone who is sick whom you could visit or for whom you could pray?

A Verse to Remember:

"A cheerful heart is a good medicine" (Prov. 17:22).

4

My Cat*

I sure like my cat, Lord.
She always seems to understand me.
She licks my face
    and then curls up close to me,
    and makes me feel all good inside.

Let's Talk

1. Do you have a pet?
2. What do you like about your pet?
3. How does your pet make you feel?
4. Who takes care of your pet?
5. Did your mother and father have pets? Ask them to tell you about their pets.
6. Pets are an extra gift from God to us. Boys and girls who live in poor countries don't have pets because they don't have enough money to take care of a pet. But 2 Samuel 12:1-3 tells about one poor man who had a pet. Read the passage. How do we know this man loved his pet very much?
7. We don't want to take our pets for granted, but we should be extra thankful for them. Why are you thankful for your pet?

A Verse to Remember:

"Every good endowment and every perfect gift is from above" (James 1:17).

---

* If you do not have a pet, you may want to go on to the next chapter.

5

Choosing Up

Dear God,
We "chose up" sides again today at school.
I hate when we do!
I can't run fast.
I can't throw far.
I'm no good at anything,
    so I'm almost always the last one to get picked.
Do you know how it feels
    to have everyone else chosen before you, Lord?
It's terrible, Terrible, TERRIBLE!
I hate school!

Let's Talk

1. Do you "choose up" at school?
    a. Who gets chosen first?
    b. Do kids get chosen only for how good they are at sports, or sometimes do they get chosen because the kids doing the choosing like them?
    c. When do you get chosen?
    d. How do you feel about that?
2. Every person needs to be able to do something well. When we can do something well, we feel good. We call this good self-esteem, or liking ourselves. It is very important to like ourselves.

Parents know it is important that we are able to do some things well, so they encourage us to be on sports teams or to learn to play the piano or some musical instrument. They also like to teach us how to do certain jobs very well. Learning these things helps our self-esteem.
    a. What things can you do well?

b. What things would you like to learn to do well?

3. God has given all of us one particular gift. If we use this gift cheerfully, we shall find that after a while when "choosing up" time comes, we will be chosen more quickly because those choosing us enjoy being with us. We read about this in 1 Corinthians 12:28; it's the gift of helping.

Why don't we begin right away to look for ways to be helpers? And then next week we can discuss how it feels to be helpers.

4. The next time you have a chance to choose, how about choosing first someone who always gets chosen last?

a. How will both of you feel then?

b. How will your parents feel when you tell them about it?

A Verse to Remember:

"Rejoice with those who rejoice, weep with those who weep. Live in harmony with one another" (Rom. 12:15).

6

When Parents Argue

Mother and Dad talked loudly to each other last night.
It scares me when they do, Lord.
I went to my room but left the door open
    so I could listen.
After a while it got quiet,
    so I went out and peeked.
Dad had his arms around Mother
    and was kissing her,
    and she was crying.
It sure made me feel funny.
I thought a lot about it after I went to bed;
    I guess it's all right if they talk loudly,
    as long as they kiss at the end.
Do you feel that way about it too, Lord?

Let's Talk

1. Do you think it's all right for Mother and Dad to disagree and argue once in a while?
    a. How do you feel while they are arguing?
    b. How do you feel when they kiss and hug each other again?
2. Ask Mom and Dad how they feel while they are arguing and how they feel afterwards?
3. Why is it hard sometimes to talk about things without getting upset and crying or getting loud?

A Verse to Remember:

"Blessed are the peacemakers, for they shall be called sons of God" (Matt. 5:9).

7

My Bossy Big Sister

Dear God,
Sometimes when Mom and Dad go out,
    they leave my big sister in charge to baby-sit us.
She won't let us eat our food in front of the TV,
    and she won't let us have all the cookies we want,
    and she won't let us stay up late.
Shucks! If she didn't say anything, Mom and Dad would never
    know.
She gets to stay up late.
Why can't we?

Let's Talk

1. What are some of the things about which brothers and sisters in your family disagree?

2. Exchange shoes with someone else in your family and walk around in those shoes. How does it feel?

3. Now play a game. Pretend you are someone in your family with whom you argue. Have someone else pretend to be you. Act out a situation like the one described in the prayer above. Choose something you argue about. Do this with two or three different situations. What did you learn from doing this?

A Verse to Remember:

"Let each of you look not only to his own interests, but also to the interests of others" (Phil. 2:4).

What does this verse mean, and how can you put it to work in your everyday life?

8

When Kids Tease Me

I get so mad
    when some of the kids yell,
    "Hey! who set your hair on fire?"
    or,
    "Want us to dump water on your head to put out the fire?"
It makes me so mad, Jesus!
I can't help if it I have red hair!
One day we were playing ball,
    and one of the guys started in on me.
Dad was listening.
When the fellows walked away,
    Dad asked quietly,
    "Why did the captain of your team choose you, Son?"
"Because I can hit," I muttered. "Everyone knows that."
"Right," Dad said. "So get out there now and hit!"
I did, and the other kids' cheering
    drowned out the bully-kid's heckling.
As I crossed home plate, I thought,
    I know now what to do when I feel angry—
    hit the ball.
Hitting the ball
    is better than punching the kid's nose, isn't it, Lord?

Let's Talk

1. Feelings of anger are difficult, uncomfortable feelings. What do kids say to you that makes you angry?

2. What do you do when you get angry?

3. What are some things that you can do that won't hurt others, but which will help you get anger out of your system?

4. Suppose you were teased and suppose you didn't hit the ball, but struck out. How would you feel then?

5. Why do you think others tease you?

6. Sometimes teasing is a kind of scratchy friendliness—people tease because they really like you. Other times people tease because they don't like themselves or something is bothering them. Thinking about why other people tease us can be helpful.

A Verse to Remember:

"Repay no one evil for evil" (Rom. 12:17).

9

A Band-Aid for a Broken Heart

Mom left home yesterday morning
    to go to a convention for four whole days.
"My heart'll break," I told her when I left for school.
When I came home, she was gone,
    but at bedtime
    I found a silly old Band-aid on my pillow
    and a note that said,
    "Here's a Band-aid for your broken heart. Love, Mom."
I snorted.

This morning Dad came and woke me up
    because Mom was on the phone.
She asked me, "Did you find the Band-aid?"
"Yup!" I said.
"Did it help?"
"Nope!"
"No?" She was surprised. "Why not?"
"It wasn't big enough," I said.
I heard her chuckle, and then she said,
    "If I weren't 3,000 miles away, I'd squeeze you so hard
    you'd yell, 'Help!' "
"That'd be better than a Band-aid," I said.

Let's Talk

1. How do you feel when Mom or Dad are away from home for a few days?

a. What helps when Mom or Dad have to be away from you?

b. Ask Mom and Dad how they feel when their work takes them away from home.

2. It's natural to feel lonely when we are separated from those whom we love.

Read Exodus 2:1-10. Who took care of baby Moses when his parents couldn't hide him any longer?

3. Read 1 Samuel 1:20-28 and 2:11. Who took care of the boy Samuel when it was time for him to live in the temple and learn to be a priest?

4. God has given us many people to care for us. Even if something should happen to your parents, God will take care of you. Ask your parents. Maybe they have already made arrangements for this so you can feel safe and secure even now.

A Verse to Remember:

"[God] has said, 'I will never fail you nor forsake you' " (Heb. 13:5).

10

My Friend's Parents Are Getting a Divorce

Brent's mother and dad aren't going to live together anymore,
   Jesus.
Brent says his stomach hurts.
He wonders what will happen to him.
I feel sorry for Brent, Lord.
Take care of him, won't you?
Show me what I can do to help him.
And please, help my mom and dad to want to stay together.

Let's Talk

1. One of the ways you can be a good friend to someone is to just listen to him. Having someone to talk to helps the other person, even if there isn't anything you can do.

    a. Do you have any friends whose parents are getting a divorce?

    b. Have you listened quietly to them?

    c. Take a moment and imagine what you would feel like if your parents were getting a divorce. What differences would it make in your life?

2. Can you tell your friend about someone who is living in a one-parent home and is well cared for and happy?

3. Do you ever worry that your mother and dad might get divorced?

4. Sometimes when a family is going through a divorce, they get so confused and upset that they can't even pray. But we can pray for them. Turn to Mark 2:1-12. Read the story of the man who couldn't get near Jesus because he was paralyzed. But he had some friends who cared enough to carry him to Jesus; and Jesus healed him. We can carry our friends to Jesus in prayer. If you have some friends who are hurting because their parents have divorced, why not pray right now for them?

A Verse to Remember:

"Have no anxiety about anything, but in everything by prayer and supplication with thanksgiving let your requests be made known to God" (Phil. 4:6).

11

When Mother Cries

I found my mother crying, Lord.
It makes me feel funny when she cries.
"I've got something in my eye," she said.
And I said, "Oh, yeah?"
"All right! So what?" she said. "I let *you* cry sometimes,
    don't I?"
I guess it's all right that she cries too, Lord.
Only don't let it happen too often.

Let's Talk

1. Why do people cry?
2. Why do you cry?
3. Ask Mother why she cries.
4. How does Mother feel after crying?
5. What does crying do for us?
6. Have you ever been so happy you've cried?
7. Does Dad cry?
8. If Dad doesn't, why doesn't he?
9. Do you think men shouldn't cry?
10. Look up these verses: Matthew 26:75; Luke 19:41; John 11:35. What do these verses tell us about men crying?
11. Why do we feel uncomfortable when people cry?
    a. Is it because we don't know how to act or what to say?
    b. What might be the best thing to do if someone starts to cry in front of you?
12. What helps you if you are crying?
13. Is there a time to stop crying? Give examples.

A Verse to Remember:

"God will wipe away every tear from their eyes" (Rev. 7:17).

12

I Feel Sorry

Robyn and I were riding our new bikes.
    Robyn's bike hit a curb
    and crashed.
His knee was bleeding,
    so I ran home
    and brought water to wash the cut,
    and a big Band-aid to put on it.

Robyn said that my caring
   helped the pain as much as
      the medicine I put on it.
Friends are for caring, aren't they, Lord?

Let's Talk

1. When a friend gets hurt, how do you feel?
2. What do you do so your friend will know how you feel?
3. Can you recall a time when you got hurt?
   a. Who helped you?
   b. What did they do?
4. Read Luke 10:30-37.
   a. What two kinds of people saw the man who needed help?
   b. How did the one who cared show that he cared?
   c. Which one did Jesus speak highly of?

A Verse to Remember:

"Do not neglect to do good and to share what you have, for such sacrifices are pleasing to God" (Heb. 13:16).

13

I Don't Like My Teacher

I don't like my teacher, Lord.
I don't think she's fair.
She doesn't listen to us
    even when she should.
I didn't have my assignment done
    because I'd been sick,
    but she wouldn't listen to me.
And when I can't understand something,
    she doesn't take time to explain.
Going to school sure isn't much fun, Lord,
    when you don't like your teacher.

Let's Talk

1. Not very often, but once in a while, we get a teacher we don't like.
    a. Have you ever had a teacher you don't like?
    b. What didn't you like about that teacher?
2. Can Mother and Dad recall having a teacher they didn't like?
    a. Why?
    b. What did they do about the problem?
3. In what ways can parents help you get along with someone you don't like?
4. What can we do if there is someone we don't like?
    a. A man named J. B. Phillips said once that if you begin to treat that person as though you liked him, after a while you will discover that you really do like him.
    b. Do you agree with this or not?

c. What are some of the things you could do for someone you dislike, to show kindness to him? Think of some *specific* things.

A Verse to Remember:

"Let us then pursue the things that make for peace" (Rom. 14:19, NEB).

14

How Do I Know God Has Forgiven Me?

Dear God,
I don't know what got into me at the store
   to make me take that pen
   and slip it into my pocket.
My face burned
   when the lady at the check-out counter asked,
     "Shall I ring up the pen in your pocket?"
And I felt sick when she called Mom
   and asked her to come down to the store.
I wished I could crawl off somewhere and hide.
I asked the lady at the store to forgive me.
"We'll let it go this time," she said.
Mom was angry, but she was sad too.
She cried when we got home,
   and then I felt worse than ever.
I've asked Mom and Dad and God to forgive me.
They didn't say anything,
   and I don't feel forgiven.
Dear God, I want to feel forgiven!
It sure would help.

Let's Talk

   1. Turn to 1 John 1:9. This verse is divided into two sections.
     a. The first section that begins with "if" explains our part.
What are we to do?
     b. The second part of the verse is God's part. What will
God do?

c. Can God lie?

d. If He can't, shouldn't we believe that when we confess our sins, God forgives us?

2. Read Isaiah 43:25. In addition to forgiving us our sins, what has God promised to do?

3. Read Psalm 103:12.

a. How far does God remove our sins from us?

b. Should we remember them then?

c. Corrie ten Boom has said that God throws our forgiven sins into the depths of the sea, and then puts up a sign that says, "No fishing!"

4. Three things can help us when we have trouble believing God has forgiven us.

a. It helps to have somebody *say* to us: "I have forgiven you and God has forgiven you."

b. It helps when in prayer we say, "Thank you, God, that you have forgiven me."

c. It helps to remember that our feelings do not determine whether or not we are forgiven. God's Word says we *are* forgiven. If God's Word says so, that's enough.

5. Do you keep remembering some specific thing for which you wonder if you've been forgiven?

a. Then, with your family, confess it and thank God that He has forgiven you.

b. Then let the family members say to you: "God has forgiven you."

c. You may respond with, "Praise the Lord!" or "I accept God's forgiveness," or "I am glad God has forgiven me."

A Verse to Remember:

"I am He [God] who blots out your transgressions for my own sake, and I will not remember your sins" (Isa. 43:25).

15

Fatty-Fatty!

I can't stand it, Lord!
It seems wherever I go,
    kids yell, "Here comes Fatso!"
    or, "Watch out! Don't let Tubs sit on that chair!"
I know I'm fat,
    but I can't help it.
I'm hungry.
When you're hungry,
    you have to eat, don't you?
Still I don't like to be fat.
I'd rather be thin.
But I like to eat.
What can I do, Lord?

Let's Talk

1. All of us eat for different reasons. Why do you eat? Because it's a habit? Because you like the taste of food? Because you're hungry? Because you're sad or worried or lonely or bored? Or because you see some tempting, delicious-looking food on TV?

2. Most of the time we eat because we're hungry. And usually we can depend on our appetites to tell us when our body has had enough. Our appetite (we could call it an "appestat") should work like a thermostat. But sometimes our "appestat" doesn't work right. It keeps on giving hunger signals when it shouldn't. This may happen, for example, if the food we eat is high in calorie count but not bulky enough to be filling. Or maybe we don't pay any attention to our "appestat." We just eat and eat.

If you can't trust your "appestat," you can certainly trust

your scale. Your scale will tell you whether you are shoveling more food into your body than it needs for fuel and energy.

3. Once we start to eat more than we should, or to eat the wrong foods, it isn't easy to stop. Take a few moments and have your family discuss your eating habits. Should some changes be made?

4. Do you know someone who is overweight?

    a. How do you think this person feels?

    b. How can you help that person?

A Verse to Remember:

"Do you not know that your body is a temple of the Holy Spirit within you, which you have from God? You are not your own; you were bought with a price. So glorify God in your body" (1 Cor. 6:19, 20).

16

I Want to Tell the World

I clap my hands and stamp my feet.
I twirl and dance and shout for joy.
Praise the Lord!
Oh, praise the Lord!

I want to tell the world!
I want to tell my neighborhood!
I want to tell my friends at school
    that God loves all of us!

Let's Talk

1. Have you ever felt so loved by God that you wanted to tell everybody?

    a. What caused you to feel that way?

    b. What kind of a feeling was it?

2. Can Mother and Dad recall a specific instance when they felt God had been so good to them that they wanted to tell everybody?

3. Read John 1:35-46.

    a. What do you think prompted Andrew to tell Simon Peter, and Philip to tell Nathanael, about Jesus?

    b. Whom have you told about Jesus?

    c. How did you feel when you told them?

    d. What was Nathanael's first answer to Philip? (vs. 46).

    e. What did Philip say in reply? (vs. 46).

4. In prayer, remember by name someone whom you wish would learn to know about Jesus' love so he or she would love Jesus in return.

A Verse to Remember:

"Go therefore and make disciples of all nations" (Matt. 28:19).

17

The Teacher's Note

I'm in trouble, Lord.
I threw away the note my teacher asked me to give to my parents,
    and now she's asking for their answer.
What do I do now, Lord?
Can you help me?
I think the note was about my homework that isn't getting done.
I'm scared to tell Mom and Dad what I did.
Will you help me?
And will you help them understand?
Please?

Let's Talk

1. Have you ever tried to hide something from your parents?
    a. Why?
    b. How did you feel when you were hiding it?
    c. In the end, did Mom and Dad find out or did you tell them?
    d. What happened then?
    e. How did you feel when it was over?
2. Now it's Mom and Dad's turn to answer questions.
    a. How do you feel when you know one of the children is hiding something from you?
    b. How do you feel when they tell you they have done something that displeases you?

A Verse to Remember:

"Confess your sins to one another, and pray for one another, that you may be healed" (James 5:16).

("Healed" also has the meaning of being made whole or complete, of no longer being broken.)

18

Spilled Milk

I don't know why grown-ups get so upset about broken dishes
   or spilled milk, Jesus.
Don't they remember that they have accidents, too?

Let's Talk

1. Why do you think parents sometimes get upset because
milk is spilled? Ask them why.

2. How can children help prevent unhappy times that sometimes follow after they track in mud, walk in on rollerskates,
don't make their beds, or leave the bathroom messy?

3. Can Mother and Dad remember foolish things they did
when they were kids?

   a. Did they ever get into trouble for doing something foolish?

   b. How did their parents react when it was an accident?

4. A grandmother was visiting her grandchildren one day
when one of the children broke their mother's favorite cup. Their
mother began to scold the child, but the grandmother bent down
and helped the child pick up the broken pieces.

"There, there," she said, "it was only a cup."

We call this "getting things into perspective." The child was
already feeling terrible because of the accident, and his mother
was making him feel worse.

Usually our perspective is better if we wait a while before we
say anything or punish in any way.

Instead of scolding, what could the mother have done that
would help her child learn how to cope with future accidents?

A Verse to Remember:

"Love bears all things, believes all things, hopes all things,
endures all things" (1 Cor. 13:7).

19

How Come Dad Can Get Away with It?

I've got another problem, Lord.
When Dad spills the milk,
  Mom smiles and runs for a sponge
  and says,
  "There, there, that's all right, dear."
But when *we* spill it. . . !
Why do parents react differently to different people, Lord?
Some things are sure hard to figure out.

Let's Talk

1. When an adult spills milk, he usually isn't scolded.
  a. Why don't parents treat adults and children the same way?
  b. What do your parents have to say about this?
2. Do you think it's possible, that because they are more careful, adults don't spill milk quite as often?
3. Is it the spilled milk that irritates, or the carelessness that caused the spill, or both?
4. What can you as a family do to avoid such unpleasant situations?
  a. Should the one who made the mess help to clean it up?
  b. Should the family take turns in helping that one, instead of Mother always cleaning up the mess?
  c. Would putting less milk in the cup help?
  d. What other solutions can you think of? (Discuss other accidents besides just spilled milk.)

Verses to Remember:

"Partiality in judging is not good" (Prov. 24:23).
"Let each of us please his neighbor" (Rom. 15:2).
"Love is patient and kind" (1 Cor. 13:4).

20

Thunderstorms

I used to get so scared when it thundered, Lord.
I would shut my eyes and plug my ears
    and curl up under the blanket.
My heart would go thump, thump, thump.
Then Dad found out how I felt,
    and now when it storms,
      he comes and takes me in his arms,
      and I feel better.

He tells me how big and mighty you are,
>how you decided where the boundaries of the sea should be,
>that you commanded morning to come and the dawn to rise
>>in the east,
>that you explored the depths of the oceans
>>and know all that lies beneath the waters,
>that you know how light came to be
>and where the planets are
>and where the home of the east wind is
>and how many stars there are,
>that you tilt the water-jars of heaven and dump out rain
>>when the ground below is dust and clods.

As I listen to him telling of all your might and power,
>the storm noises outside become a percussion band:
>>the low rumbling,
>>the loud crash-bangs of thunder,
>>the sharp crackle-snap of lightning,
>>and the steady hiss of the rain.

All of them seem to cry out:
>God is mighty!
>Let us praise the Lord!

Let's Talk

1. Tell about one time when you were especially frightened by a storm.

2. Have you ever experienced an earthquake? How did you feel?

3. How do you feel when it storms?

4. Can Mother and Dad each remember one time when they were really scared?

5. What helps you feel better when you get scared?

6. Turn to Matthew 8:23-27 and read about a time when Jesus' disciples were afraid in a storm. What did they do?

7. How can we be sure Jesus will take care of us regardless of what happens?

A Verse to Remember:

"Fear not, for I am with you, be not dismayed, for I am your God; I will strengthen you, I will help you, I will uphold you with my victorious right hand" (Isa. 41:10).

21

The Bully on Our Street

I hate that big guy on our street.
He's so mean!
I have to walk way around his house on my way home from school
    so I won't meet him.
I'm afraid he'll beat me up.
I wish I could tell my dad about him.
Were you ever afraid, Lord?

Let's Talk

1. People are mean for many reasons. When they are mean to us, it may help to ask ourselves, "Why do they act like that?"

2. Joseph's brothers were so mean to him that they sold him to some people who took him to a far-off country. Read the story in Genesis 37:1-28.

    a. Look at verse 2. What did Joseph do that probably made his brothers angry?

    b. Look at verse 4. Why else did they hate him?

    c. Why did they hate him when Joseph told them about his dream?

    d. Would it have been wiser if Joseph had kept quiet?

    e. Do you know any kids who brag?

    f. How do you feel when somebody brags?

    g. Look at verse 19. Instead of calling Joseph their brother, what did his brothers call him? What were they still feeling angry about?

3. Sometimes, however, we suffer innocently from other people's anger. We haven't done anything wrong against them, but they take their anger out on us, because we happen to be close by

or because we are smaller than they. When that happens we need to forgive them and help them.

    a. Has anyone been mean to you?

    b. Are you afraid of anyone?

    c. Can you guess why they are mean to you?

    d. Spend a moment praying for someone who has been mean to you. This will be hard to do. If you find you can't do it right away, ask Jesus to help you.

A Verse to Remember:

"Love your enemies and pray for those who persecute you" (Matt. 5:44).

22

My Teacher

My teacher's sure pretty, Jesus.
Almost as pretty as my mother.
I think I'll marry her when I grow up.
I'll take her to live
    on that nice big farm outside of town.
Wouldn't that be nice, Lord?

Let's Talk

1. Is this young boy's wish to marry his teacher a pretend wish or a real wish?
2. All of us play pretend some of the time.
    a. Do you have a pretend friend?
    b. What do you do together?
    c. Do you sometimes pretend to be somebody else other than yourself?
    d. Who do you pretend to be?
3. Can Mother and Dad remember playing pretend?
4. Sometimes we get so engrossed in playing pretend, we forget what's for real. How do we feel when we come back to the real world?
5. Most of the time we play pretend just for fun, but sometimes we play pretend to escape. Can you think of an example of this?
6. Sometimes boys or girls whose parents are divorced or whose mother or father has died play pretend. They pretend that what happened really hasn't happened.
    a. Why do you think they play pretend in this way?
    b. How can we help them?

A Verse to Remember:

"My grace is sufficient for you" (2 Cor. 12:9).

23

Our Silly Cat

Lord, our silly cat
  sure made a fuss last night.
She walked into Mother's room
  where the long mirror Mother had just bought
  was propped against the wall.
Our cat came face to face with her own reflection.
She hunched her back
  and spat
  and snarled
  and her tail puffed up thick and fat and stiff.
Silly cat!
She thought she'd met an enemy! But the enemy was only her-
  self.
Sometimes I wonder if I'm like that cat.

Let's Talk

Jesus said we should love others as we love ourselves. When
He said, "Love your neighbor as yourself," He implied that we
should be good and kind to ourselves. God wants us to be friends
to ourselves, not enemies.

1. When are people not good to themselves? Give examples.
2. When are you not good to yourself?
3. When are people good to themselves? Give examples.
4. When are you good to yourself?

A Verse to Remember:

"[God says] you are precious in my eyes, and honored, and I
love you" (Isa. 43:4).

24

Why Did We Have to Move?

We've sold our home, Lord.
Why did we have to move?
As we flew away on the plane,
    I asked Dad if planes can ever turn around.
I wish ours had.
We've had to move so many times.
Why?
"Dad got another promotion," Mom says.
But couldn't he have stayed at his old job,
    so we wouldn't have had to move?

Let's Talk

1. Have you ever had to move?
    a. Was it a happy experience?
    b. Or do you wish you could have stayed on where you were?
2. If your family has moved, talk about why you moved.
3. Have each member of the family tell how he or she felt about moving.
4. How do you feel now about having moved?
5. Ask your parents to explain why sometimes a family has to move because the mother's or father's employer asks them to do so. Discuss how moving can even help the family.
6. One of the first persons in the Bible who had to move was Abraham. Turn to Genesis 12:1-3.
    a. Why did Abraham have to move?
    b. How do you think he felt about going?
    c. What was the result of Abraham's move?

A Verse to Remember:

"Be strong and of good courage; be not frightened, neither be dismayed; for the Lord your God is with you wherever you go" (Josh. 1:9).

25

Sharing Rooms

Lisa and I have to share a room.
Sometimes I wish we could have separate rooms.
Then I'd have a closet all to myself,
    and I could go to bed when I wanted to,
    and I wouldn't have Lisa's mess to clean up.
But when Lisa goes
    to spend the night with Tara,
    our room is sure quiet and
    lonely;
    and I usually ask Mother
    if I can phone Nicki to come and stay with me.
So, I guess, in the end,
    sharing a room
    isn't so bad after all.

Let's Talk

1. Do you share a room?
2. What's nice about sharing a room?
3. What's not so nice about sharing a room?
4. Does sharing a room cause some disagreements and irritations between brothers and sisters in your family?
5. Ask Mother and Dad what it's like for them to share a room.
6. Turn to 2 Kings 4:8-10 and read about some people who shared their home with others.
7. With whom have you shared your home?
8. What kind of an experience was it?

A special blessing comes when we open our homes to those who need a place to stay.

A Verse to Remember:

"Do not neglect to show hospitality to strangers, for thereby some have entertained angels unawares" (Heb. 13:2).

26

Cooked-Spaghetti Knees

When our choir has to stand up in front at church and sing,
    my knees feel like cooked spaghetti.
Even if I'm in the back row, my pant legs flap as though
    a breeze were blowing.
I wonder if people can see me shaking.
I try to stand real stiff,
    but then all of a sudden I shake worse than ever.
My hands get cold and wet
    and sometimes my upper lip quivers.
"You looked like a ghost," one of the kids said to me
    last time after we sang.
Do you think there's any hope for me, Lord?
Will I ever get over it?
Sometimes I think I would like to be a preacher or a lawyer
    when I grow up,
    but how will that ever be possible with me so scared?
I look at my teachers.
They're not scared.
How did they get over it?
Lord, sometimes I think it must be nice to be a grown-up.

Let's Talk

1. There are many nice things about being a grown-up. But you don't have to wait until then to learn how to handle some things, such as being jittery in front of people.

    a. Ask Mother and Dad if they ever have to speak in front of people.

    b. Do they get nervous?

c. How do they feel?

d. What have they found helps them?

2. If you have to speak in front of a group, good preparation helps a lot. It is a good thing to write out your talk. Then you know exactly what you are going to do or say.

Practicing in front of some of your friends or your parents helps too. Thinking of the words you are going to say or sing, and saying and singing those words with all your heart also helps. It helps, too, to pick one or two friends in the audience who will smile at you and make you feel good. All these things help you forget yourself, and then you won't feel so frightened.

3. Turn to Exodus 4:10-16. Ask someone to read this.

Moses, who was a great man of God, told the Lord he couldn't speak. God told Moses He would help him, but Moses couldn't believe it. So, in the end, God gave Aaron to Moses to help him. But in the years that followed, Aaron caused Moses much trouble and sorrow. Maybe it would have been better if Moses had trusted God to help him. It is better for us to accept responsibility, even if we are scared, than to expect someone else to do the job.

A Verse to Remember:

"When I am afraid, I put my trust in thee" (Ps. 56:3).

27

The Rain

It's raining today, Lord.
I love the rain.
I tip my head back,
    and the rain splashes down all over my face.
It's cool, but not cold,
    and soft and smooth
    and it feels so funny dripping off my chin.
The rain makes me feel
    clean, clean, clean—
    way down deep inside, too.
I love the rain, Lord.
Thank you for it.

Let's Talk

1. When was the last time you felt the rain on your face? How did it feel?

2. Read Job 37:5-13. Discuss what you think verse 13 means.

3. In some parts of the country it rains only a few inches a year. People who live in these areas are always glad when it rains, because then all the bushes and trees and houses get washed clean.

    a. Sometimes we might get the feeling of not being clean inside. What do you think would cause us to feel this way?

    b. How do we get back that clean feeling?

A Verse to Remember:

"Wash me thoroughly from my iniquity, and cleanse me from my sin" (Ps. 51:2).

(Iniquity means I can't go "straight" by myself; I am twisted and warped. I need God's help to go straight and be honest.)

28

I Hate Myself, Lord!

I hate myself, Lord!
Why was I born with freckles
    and with eyes so weak that I have to wear glasses?
All the kids at school yell and call me "Four-eyes."
I don't want to look in the mirror.
My teeth are even coming in crooked.
What if I have to wear braces?
I wish I were somebody else
    other than me.
What can I do?
Look at my sister, Lord.
She's pretty.
She doesn't have freckles,
    and she doesn't wear glasses.
Her teeth are nice and even.
Why can't I be like her, huh?
It's not fair!

Let's Talk

1. Do you think anyone is completely satisfied with the way he or she looks? Talk about it.
    a. What doesn't your mother like about the way she looks?
    b. What doesn't your dad like about the way he looks?
    c. What about the others in your family?
2. Now let's talk about something else.
    a. What do *you* like most about your mother? If there are several children in the family, have each one answer these questions.

b. What do you like about your dad?

c. What do you like about your friends?

d. Ask Mother and Dad to tell what they like best about each one in your family.

3. Which is more important: what we look like or the kind of persons we are?

4. What kind of a person would you like to be?

5. Close your eyes and sit for a moment, picturing yourself as the kind of a person you'd like to be. Then go around the family circle and pray. Ask God to help you accept your physical looks. Ask Him also to help you become the kind of person He wants you to be.

A Verse to Remember:

"Will the pot contend with the potter. . . ? Will the clay ask the potter what he is making? or his handiwork say to him, 'You have no skill'?" (Isa. 45:9, NEB).

29

Going-to-the-Hospital Worries

I have to go to the hospital tomorrow, Lord,
  and I'm scared!
My stomach feels all mixed up inside.
It's awful! Will you help me?
I think if I knew Mother could stay with me,
  it might help.
And if I knew exactly what they are going to do to me,
  and whether or not it will hurt,
  or how much,
  I wouldn't be so worried.
Would that make my stomach feel better, I wonder?

Let's Talk

1. How many in your family have been sick and had to stay in a hospital? Tell what it was like.

2. If no one in your family stayed in a hospital, play a game. Pretend that the doctor has told you that you must have an appendicitis operation. You are in the doctor's office. Let your parents be the "nurse" and the "doctor." Ask them any questions you want to about your upcoming hospital stay and surgery, and they will answer you.

3. Now pretend that one of you has broken an arm. Act out what would happen then. You'll need both parents and a "doctor" and a "nurse."

4. Talk about what would happen in your family if Mother or Dad had to go to the hospital.

5. Now imagine you are a child needing surgery, but you are in a country where there is no doctor or hospital nearby. In such a situation, what would you talk about? How would you feel?

6. Hospitals and doctors and nurses are wonderful gifts God has given us. Thank God now for them and also for the assurance that when we are ill, Jesus, the greatest physician of all, will care for us.

A Verse to Remember:

"Bless the Lord, O my soul . . . who heals all your diseases" (Ps. 103:2, 3).

30

Big Brother

Dear God,
I sure like my big brother, Dan!
When he walks with me to school,
    I'm not afraid of anybody!
And when I watch him hit home runs,
    I yell my head off.
Most of the time Dan is nice to me.
Once in a while, though, we fight.
Like when he catches me messin' in his drawers,
    or using his hair dryer.
But I don't like *him* messin' up my hair
    or spraying me with the water hose, either.
But most of the time we get along just fine.
I sure like my big brother, Lord!

Let's Talk

1. What do you like about your brothers and sisters?
2. What *don't* you like about your brothers and sisters?
3. When do you enjoy your brothers most?
4. When do you enjoy your sisters most?
5. What do you argue about with your brothers or sisters?
6. How do you make up after arguing?
7. When someone else says something unkind about your brothers or sisters, how do you feel?
8. When Jesus called His disciples, He chose two sets of brothers. Who were they? (See Matthew 10:2.)
9. What two sisters were followers of Jesus? (See John 11:5.)
10. Whom do we read about in Genesis 45:4 who forgave his

brothers who had been mean to him? How did he help his brothers (45:9-11)?

11. Can you think of a time when a brother or sister shared your troubles and helped you? How did they help?

12. Can Mother and Dad tell of a time when their brothers or sisters helped them? Ask them to tell you about it.

A Verse to Remember:

"A brother is born to help in time of need" (Prov. 17:17, TLB).

31

But Nobody Else Has To!

Dear God,
I don't understand why parents make their kids do things
   that none of the other kids do.
Mom made me carry an umbrella to school today,
   and I hated it!
"You're just getting over a cold,
   and it's going to rain," she said.
But who cares if it rains a little?
I hate it when Mom makes me do things like this!

Let's Talk

1. Can Mother and Dad remember something their parents made them do that they didn't want to do? Have them tell about it.

2. Do your parents ever ask you to do things you don't want to do? Give some examples.

   a. Now let's each talk about those times. Let's give the kids a chance to talk first. Mother and Dad are not to respond until the kids are all through telling why they think they don't have to do certain things.

   b. Now let Mother and Dad tell why they asked the children to do these things. The children should listen (and not interrupt) and really try to understand.

3. Sometimes when children say, "*No one* else does that," do you think there is a possibility that they are exaggerating?

4. Read Ephesians 6:1, 2. Do you think one reason God gave this command was because parents can see "farther" than children?

5. Read Ephesians 6:4. What do you think this verse means?

6. Do we always have to be like everybody else, or is it all right once in a while to be different?

7. Read Matthew 26:69-75.

   a. Do you think that when the maid spoke to Peter, she did so in a teasing voice?

   b. Why was Peter afraid to admit that he was one of Jesus' friends?

   c. Was he afraid to be different from all the others around? Why?

d. Instead of admitting he was one of Jesus' disciples, what did Peter do?

e. How did he feel about this afterwards?

f. In later years, what did he write in one of his letters (1 Pet. 3:14)?

8. Sometimes even after we talk these things over, we discover that in our hearts we really don't want to obey our parents. Then we need to ask God to give us willing and obedient spirits. He will help us.

A Verse to Remember:

"Uphold me with a willing spirit" (Ps. 51:12).

32

I Love to Sing!

I sure like to sing, Lord!
When our choir sings "God bless America,"
I sing as loud as I can, and I think,
I sure love my country.
It chokes me up.

Let's Talk

1. What are some of the good things we enjoy because we live in this country? See how many you can name. Have someone write them down as you name them.
2. Do you know the name of the governor of your state?
3. Do you know the names of your legislators?
4. If you live in a city, do you know the name of the mayor?
5. Try to imagine what it must be like to be President.
   a. How do you think he feels?
   b. How do you think his wife feels?
   c. How do you think his children feel?
6. Look up 1 Timothy 2:1, 2.
   a. What does God's Word say we should do for our leaders?

b. Spend time now obeying that command. Remember people by name when you pray for them. Each person can choose one or two leaders to pray for.

Verses to Remember:

"First of all, then, I urge that supplications, prayers, intercessions, and thanksgivings be made for all men, for kings and all who are in high positions" (1 Tim. 2:1, 2).

33

Sometimes I Don't Like My Parents

Lord, sometimes I almost hate my parents.
I wish I could tell them how I feel.
I think I'd feel better.
But I'm afraid they would stop loving me.
Or they might feel hurt.
Is it better that I don't say the words?
But what do I do with these feelings? They just come.
They come
    when I feel my parents just don't understand me.
    when I feel my parents aren't being fair.
    when I think my parents judge before they listen.
    when they punish too hard for a little mistake,
    or when they nag and nag and never forget if I've done
       something wrong.
Why is it sometimes so hard to get along with parents, Lord?

Let's Talk

1. Lisa stormed out the house, slamming the door and yelling, "I hate you!" She wanted to go to a movie with her friends, but her dad had said no.

I wish he'd die! Lisa thought as her feet bore down hard on the pedals of her bike.

Two days later the principal at Lisa's school sent for her to come to the office. She greeted Lisa kindly, then walked around, straightening the shade of the lamp on her desk and picking lint off the carpet. She finally told Lisa there had been an accident.

Lisa's father was in the hospital. Two days later he died.

Lisa didn't cry, but she didn't want to talk about her father's death, either. Inside she felt terrible, certain that she was guilty of her father's death, though she really loved him very much. She began to have dreams about monsters and ghosts.

Lisa's mother was grieving so much that she didn't pay much attention to Lisa or notice how quiet and pale she had become. But a teacher at school did. She spent many hours talking to Lisa. Then Lisa began to understand that many people have feelings of both hate and love for those whom they really care about. We call these ambivalent, or upside-down, mixed-up feelings. To feel that way isn't unusual.

Lisa also recognized that she hadn't killed her father. She learned that no one else was blaming her for her father's death. Only *she* had such thoughts.

When Lisa understood and accepted this, and asked God to forgive her for her attitude toward her father, she felt better.

2. When do you get "hate" feelings or angry feelings toward your parents?

3. When do they get "hate" feelings toward you?

4. Does this mean you don't love each other?

5. What is a good way to handle these feelings?

6. Lisa felt guilty when her father died. Sometimes children whose parents divorce feel guilty. They think they have caused the divorce. What would you say to a friend who says to you, "My parents are getting a divorce, and I'm sure I'm to blame"?

A Verse to Remember:

"Be angry but do not sin; do not let the sun go down on your anger" (Eph. 4:26).

34

I'm Glad We're Moving

Lord, so many people say to me,
  "You must be sad that you're moving."
But actually, God, I'm not.
I'm glad.
I haven't had many friends here.
Mom and Dad have cars
    and can go to their friends
    wherever their friends live.
Kids like me are stuck with the kids in the neighborhood.
Don't parents ever think of this?
There haven't been many friends here for me, Lord.
I'm counting on you to find friends for me in our new place.

Let's Talk

1. Moving is always an adventure. Moving means going to a
new school and getting to know the people who live next door.
    a. Have you ever moved?
    b. How did you feel about it?
    c. What did you like about it?
    d. What didn't you like about it?
    e. How did Mother feel about moving?
    f. How did Father feel about moving?
    g. How did you make new friends?
2. When we are anxious or when we have a new need, it's a
good feeling to know that we can talk to God about it. Let's look
up and read some of God's promises to us: Philippians 4:6, 7;
Philippians 4:19; Hebrews 4:15, 16.
3. Spend some time in prayer, telling God about your special
needs.

A Verse to Remember:

"For we have not a high priest who is unable to sympathize with our weaknesses, but one who in every respect has been tempted as we are, yet without sinning" (Heb. 4:15).

35

I Wish Dad Lived with Us

Dear God,
I wish my mom and dad lived together!
Oh, I like when Dad comes to pick me up on Saturdays.
He always plans special things for us to do,
    but sometimes I'd rather just have him here at home
    doing nothing special—
    just being here.
But I hated it when Mom and Dad fought all the time.
I think maybe they're both happier now,
    though sometimes in a sort of sad way.
And I know they both love me.
I wish they could live together again without fighting, Lord.

Let's Talk

1. Are your mom and dad divorced?
    a. What differences has this made for all of you?
    b. How do you feel about life now?
    c. How does Mother feel?
    d. How does Dad feel?
    e. What things are hard for you?
    f. What can your family do to help now?
    g. What things are better for you now?
    h. What is hard for Mother?
    i. Can you help her? How?
    j. What is hard for Dad? Who can help him and how?
2. Read the promises God has given us in Isaiah 26:3 and Jeremiah 7:23. What things would you like to pray for now?

A Verse to Remember:

"My God will supply every need of yours according to his riches in glory in Christ Jesus" (Phil. 4:19).

36

My Dog, Prince, Died

I can't tell you how awful I feel, Lord.
My dog, Prince, died.
I know he was old and had to die,
    but *why* did he have to?
He didn't look that worn out to me.
I feel so awfully sad.
I hurt inside.
Mom asked me if I wanted to stay home from school.
"I'm too sad to stay home," I said.
Couldn't she understand that?

I wish Mom wouldn't keep talking
    about Prince, Lord.
I don't want to think about him—
    only I do, all the time.
I don't ever want another dog—
    never, Never, NEVER.

Dad came home from work and said he had a surprise for me
    out in the car.
I ran out to see,
    and a little puppy was jumping up against the window,
    barking and barking.
He chewed me all over when I let him out,
    and I felt all mixed up inside.
I guess I was glad to have him,
    but I still felt angry
    that I couldn't have my old Prince
    instead of this noisy puppy.

It's getting better, though.
My puppy still gets tangled up in my feet
    when I come home from school,
    and at night he walks all over my face,
    instead of lying still on the floor beside me
        like Prince used to do.
But it's nice to have him,
    and I don't miss Prince quite so much anymore.
It's all right not to miss Prince quite so much,
    isn't it?
Prince would want me to be happy with my new puppy,
    wouldn't he?
They'd play together,
    and Prince would have fun, too, wouldn't he?
Mom says it's all right to feel happy.
Do you agree, Lord?

Let's Talk

1. Has a pet of yours ever died? How did you feel?

2. Can Mother and Dad remember when a pet of theirs died? How did they feel?

3. Why do we sometimes feel angry when a pet of ours dies or when someone we love dies?

4. What happens to us *physically* when we die?

5. In what way are people different from animals?

6. It's all right to feel sad when we lose someone or something we've cared about very much. We might even feel angry. But God understands how we feel. He will help us so that after a while we'll feel happy again.

A Verse to Remember:

"He has sent me to heal the brokenhearted" (Luke 4:18, TLB).

37

Who Says I Can Get All A's?

I had all A's on my report card, except for two B's.
"You could do better than that," Mother said.
Who does she think I am anyway?
The genius of the class?
Jason got three B's, but she didn't say anything to him.
"The kid sitting behind me disturbs me," I said.
He doesn't really, but I had to say something.
I hate report cards!
Why are grades so important?
Next time I think I'll get all C's.

Let's Talk

1. What kind of conversations take place in your house when you come home with your report cards?

2. Let's play a game. The children are to be the father and mother, and Father and Mother are to pretend they are the children. Now act out what happens when the children bring home their report cards.

3. How do you feel when your parents say, "You could do better"?

4. Ask Mother and Dad how *they* feel when they say, "You could do better."

5. In most schools, grades show how a student is doing in comparison with what other students are doing. What difference would it make if grades showed how you are doing in comparison with what *you* can do?

6. When most parents say, "You can do better," they do not mean, "You can do better than all the other kids in your class and get an A." You probably can't do better than *all* the other kids. And even if you could, sooner or later you would meet someone who would do better than you in something. None of us can do the best in everything, nor does anyone expect us to. But we can do the best *we* can.

Parents don't mean to be unkind. Rather, because parents love their children, they want them to do the best they can.

7. How do you feel when you have done the best you can most of the time? (None of us does our best *all* of the time.)

    a. Why should we want to do our best?

    b. Whom are we helping by doing so?

8. What attitude is reflected when we say, "My parents didn't like it because I didn't get all A's, so next time I'll get C's"?

A Verse to Remember:

"Whatever your hand finds to do, do it with your might" (Eccles. 9:10).

38

Why Can't I Do Wrong and Feel Good?

Dear God,
Can you tell me something?
When Mom and Dad went out tonight,
    they told our big sister,
        "No TV tonight. There's nothing good on."
But we talked our sister
    into letting us watch a real scary show.
But why is it
    that even if Mom and Dad don't find out about it,
    I still don't feel good that we did it?

Let's Talk

1. What is the answer to the above question?

2. Sometimes we think we shouldn't do something because we might be punished for it. But what happens inside us when we do wrong that makes us feel just as miserable as being punished?

3. Read Psalm 32:3, 4. What did the Psalmist say happened to him when he covered up his sin?

4. Read Psalm 51:1-12. Note verses 8 and 12. How did the Psalmist expect to feel after he confessed his sin?

5. Is there something you have kept hidden from God that you should confess?

6. Is there something you should confess to your parents or to someone else?

7. If we confess our sins, what does God promise to do? (See 1 John 1:9.)

8. Have a time of prayer together.

A Verse to Remember:

"If we confess our sins, he is faithful and just, and will forgive our sins and cleanse us from all unrighteousness" (1 John 1:9).

39

Having Someone with Me Helps

I was supposed to go to the dentist today,
    and when Mother reminded me,
    I felt scared inside.
Then the telephone rang.
The receptionist at the dentist's office asked
    if I could come Saturday morning instead.
"Since I don't work on Saturdays, I'll go with you," Dad said.
Somehow I don't feel as scared anymore.
Dear God,
    Why are some things easier for me to do
    when Dad is with me?

Let's Talk

1. Can you answer the question?

2. It's natural to feel scared when you have to do something alone. Many years ago God gave a man called Joshua a job to do. Joshua felt frightened, so God gave Joshua a special promise. Read the promise in Joshua 1:5, 9.

3. Have you ever been afraid to do something and then had someone say they would help you? Tell about it.

    a. What difference did it make in the way you felt?

    b. Can Mother and Dad recall a similar experience?

4. Talk a little bit about the kind of person you like to be with.

5. Pray and thank God for certain people (name them) whom He has given to help you.

A Verse to Remember:

"Bear one another's burdens" (Gal. 6:2).

40

Why Do I Have to Go to Family Picnics?

Dear God,
Tomorrow I have to go to one of those picnics
    where all our relatives get together.
I hate those picnics, God.
I hardly know those people,
    but they tickle me under my chin,
    or they put their arm around me
    and say, "My! haven't you grown!"
    or, "You look just like your mother."
I feel so dumb.
Why do parents want us to meet all our relatives, Lord?

Let's Talk

1. Ask Mother and Dad how they would answer that question.

2. Discuss why we feel strange when we are with people we don't really know, but who act as though they know us very well.

3. In what ways can having relatives be a happy experience?

4. Play a game.

    a. Mother will name her sisters and brothers (your aunts and uncles) one by one. Then each of you write on a paper the names of the people those aunts and uncles married (if they are married) and the names of their children.

    b. Do the same for Father's sisters and brothers.

    c. How many could write all the names?

5. Collect photos of all your grandparents, aunts, uncles and

cousins. Mount these photos on a bulletin board. Then every night choose a different family and pray for each member by name.

A Verse to Remember:

"I thank my God in all my remembrance of you, always in every prayer of mine for you all making my prayer with joy" (Phil. 1:3).

41

Sometimes I Don't Want to Grow Up

Thank you, Jesus,
> that I can tell my mother everything
> and she doesn't laugh at me.

I got awfully hungry this afternoon and asked her for a sandwich.
"You're hungry because you didn't eat breakfast or lunch," she said.
"I know," I agreed. "Know why I didn't eat?"
"Why?" she asked.
"Well, 'cuz yesterday when I climbed up on your lap, you said,
> 'My! You're getting big!
> Pretty soon I won't be able to hold you on my lap anymore.'

And, you see, I *like* to sit on your lap."
Mom didn't laugh at me, Jesus.
She just pulled me onto her lap and hugged and kissed me and said,
> "That's the way growing up is.
> We want to
> and we don't want to.
> Now how about a sandwich?"

It sure tasted good, Lord,
> and I felt comfortable and good just sitting close to Mother.

I guess you'll help me when growing-up time comes.

Let's Talk

1. Feelings are funny things. Sometimes we feel big and strong. We don't think we need our parents very much. We

dream about being free and having our own house and car. We think that would be just wonderful. Then again we feel like we never want to leave our mother or father. When we are with them, we feel secure and happy. It's nice knowing they'll look after us. And it's all right to feel both ways.

2. What is good about growing up?

3. What isn't so good about growing up?

4. How do you feel about growing up?

5. Now talk about a time when you felt especially close to your mother or dad. How did it make you feel?

6. Ask your mother and dad to tell about a time when they felt very close to you and knew they loved you very much. How did that experience make them feel?

7. Ask Mother and Dad to tell you about a time when they felt very close to each other.

8. Now spend time thanking God for each other.

A Verse to Remember:

"So faith, hope, love abide, these three; but the greatest of these is love" (1 Cor. 13:13).

42

Grandma Died

Grandma died, and Dad cried.
I couldn't understand that, Lord.
I said, "If Grandma is with Jesus now,
   isn't she all right?"
"But I miss her," Dad said.
Guess I can understand that.
I miss her, too.
Sometimes I miss her a lot, and sometimes just a little.
Dad maybe misses Grandma more than I do,
   because, after all,
   he was Grandma's little boy once.
So I guess it's all right if Dad cries.
But it still makes me feel funny.
I think I'll go outside and play until Dad feels better.

Let's Talk

1. Have you ever seen your mother or father cry?
    a. Why were they crying?
    b. How did you feel?
    c. What did you do?
2. Has your grandfather or grandmother died?
    a. Ask your mother and dad how they felt when that happened.
    b. Do you remember it?
    c. How did you feel?
3. Ask your parents to tell you how they felt when one of their grandparents died.
4. One day a good friend of Jesus died. When Jesus heard the

news, He cried. Read about it in John 11:1-44. It is a beautiful story.

5. When someone we love dies, it's all right if we cry. Usually we feel better after we have cried. So if we see grown-ups crying, we shouldn't worry. Instead, we should say to ourselves, "It's good for them to cry. After a while they won't hurt as much or cry as much either."

A Verse to Remember:

"The dead in Christ will rise first; then we who are alive, who are left, shall be caught up together with them in the clouds to meet the Lord in the air; and so we shall always be with the Lord. Therefore comfort one another with these words" (1 Thess. 4:16-18).

43

Hurrah for Showers!

The water gushing
  and rushing
  and pouring over me in the shower
makes me want to sing
    LOUD!
Thank you for showers, Jesus.

Let's Talk

1. Do you enjoy taking showers or playing in the bathtub? Why?

2. God has blessed us with a sense of touch. Discuss what it would be like if we couldn't feel the things that touch us. For example, what would it be like to feed ourselves if we couldn't feel the fork we eat with, or if our mouth couldn't feel the food we put in it?

3. People with Hansen's disease, or leprosy, lose their sense of touch. They can grab a very hot kettle and not feel the heat. Because of this, they can get seriously burned without knowing it. So even when we feel pain we can be thankful, because feeling pain can prevent us from being seriously hurt.

4. What things that touch you make you feel good? (Examples: snow falling, a strong wind, a dog rubbing your leg.) Talk about this.

5. What people do you like to have touch you?

6. In Matthew 8:3; 8:15; 9:29; and 20:34, we read of Jesus touching people. Look up these verses and read them. Pretend you are one of the persons Jesus touched and tell your family how it felt when Jesus touched you.

7. Spend some time thanking God for the gift of touch.

A Verse to Remember:

"God . . . giveth us richly all things to enjoy" (1 Tim. 6:17, KJV).

44

Our Neighbor Girl

The little girl next door is sure pretty, Lord.
When I walk through the gate at school
  behind her long, shining, brown hair,
I get all shivery.

Let's Talk

1. GIRLS: What kind of boys do you like?
   BOYS: What kind of girls do you like?
2. God made boys and girls so they can feel a special love for
each other. But learning to *really* love another person usually
takes lots of time. Before two people really love each other, they
feel excited about each other. This is all right, too; it's part of the
way God made us. Usually boys and girls don't begin to have excited feelings about each other until they are twelve and thirteen,
but that's all right, too. God has a right time for everything.
   But it's good to begin early to pray that God will lead us to
the right man or woman to marry when we grow up. Getting mar-
ried is one of the most important things we do in life.
3. Ask Mother and Dad how they met each other.
   a. What did they like about each other?
   b. What kind of feelings do they have toward each other
now?
   c. Have they ever been mad at each other?
   d. What keeps them loving each other?

A Verse to Remember:

"That is why a man leaves his father and mother and is
united to his wife, and the two become one" (Gen. 2:24, NEB).

45

Smashed Bike

Jesus,
I want to thank you specially
    'cuz Dad didn't get too mad
    when he saw my smashed bike.
I know I shouldn't have left it in the street.
I'll need your help though, Lord,
    when I wash all those windows and cars
    that Dad says I'll have to wash
    to help buy a new bike.
I feel tired already.

Let's Talk

1. Have you ever broken something valuable, or had something stolen because you were careless?
    a. How did you feel?
    b. Was it easy to tell Mother and Dad about it? Explain.

2. If you were a mother or father, and one of your kids smashed up his bike, what would you say and do?

3. Now ask Mother and Father how they felt about you when you told them what had happened.
    a. Did they feel differently after a little while?
    b. Did they talk right away or did they wait a little before they decided what to do?

4. What is the difference between "punish" and "chastise"? You might have to look up those words in the dictionary. Read Hebrews 12:5-7, 11 and talk about those verses.

A Verse to Remember:

"For the Lord disciplines him whom he loves, and chastises every son whom he receives" (Heb. 12:6).

46

Leaping and Jumping

It's so much fun
   to leap and jump,
   Lord!
I feel
   as though I could
   spend all day
   leaping and run-
   ning and jump-
   ing.

Let's Talk

1. Do you sometimes have days when you feel like leaping and jumping?

   a. How do you feel on those days?

   b. What happens if you're feeling that way and you have to sit still in church or school?

c. What helps you to sit still, or can't you sit still?

2. Then, again, on certain days, do you feel like not playing or running at all? Would you rather just read or lie on your bed? You might even feel a little sad for no reason at all.

3. That's the way life is. We sometimes feel happy and full of pep. Sometimes we feel sad and want to be quiet. That's normal.

Some boys and girls, however, have problems. Some boys and girls always feel so excited they can never be still. They may even get so excited that they punch people or break things. When this happens frequently, doctors suspect that those children's brains aren't working quite like they should; their brains aren't allowing them to rest. Doctors refer to these children as being "hyperactive."

You may have some hyperactive children in your class or school. Maybe they are loud and noisy and disturb the class, or maybe they pick fights.

We must try to understand disruptive children who have problems like this. We have to be very patient with them and try not to annoy them but try to love them.

Do you know any children who have problems like this? If so, why don't you remember them and their families in prayer right now? Both they and their families have mixed-up, unhappy feelings to deal with.

A Verse to Remember:

"Love one another with brotherly affection. . . . Be constant in prayer" (Rom. 12:10, 12).

47

My Report Card Wasn't Good

My report card wasn't very good, Lord.
I waited for Mom and Dad to scold me.
They didn't.
Instead they asked, "How do *you* feel about it?"
That made me feel worse.
I guess I really should do something about it,
  but I don't know what to do.

Let's Talk

1. Sometimes when we fail, we cover up our feelings. We act smart and say, "Who cares?" Or we laugh. Or we get mad at someone else and sock them or tease them. But how do you *really* feel way deep down inside when you fail? Talk about this.

2. It's natural to feel bad or discouraged or depressed or even angry when we fail. Usually, however, we can find a way to improve.

What do you fail at? Studies at school? Sports? Making friends? Keeping your temper? Telling the truth?

3. As a family, have each person tell what his weak points are. Mother and Dad should participate, too. Explain, if you know, why you are failing.

4. What can we do to get help? One good thing to do is what we have been doing right now—talking to someone about it. We can talk to our parents, teachers, friends, or our pastor. However, it's important for us be honest and tell them exactly how we feel. We are like watermelons—people can't know what we're like

inside, or what we are feeling, if we won't allow ourselves to be "cracked open."

5. Sometimes there is something bothering us, but we feel ashamed to talk about it. When we are with those who love us, we should never have to fear to tell them *everything*. We can be assured they will love us, even if we have done something we shouldn't have done. And they will love us even if we have weaknesses.

God will help us, too. And, very often God helps us through the words and wisdom of others. That's why "talking it out" is so important.

A Verse to Remember:

"Cast all your anxieties on him, for he cares about you" (1 Pet. 5:7).

48

I Wish Dad Wasn't So Busy

Jesus, why do dads have to be so busy?
I wish my dad had time to go fishing with me.
Seems to me the three things he says most to me are:
    "I'm too busy."
    "How much does it cost?"
    "I'm too tired."
Why does it have to be this way, Lord?
Why can't parents enjoy their kids?
My mom, too, works so hard and gets so tired.
I feel bad when she's tired.
What can I do?
Can I tell them how I feel, Lord?
What would they say?
Would they understand?
Or would they interrupt me, and say,
    "I'm too busy just now"?

Let's Talk

1. Do you ever feel your mother or dad are too busy?

    a. What would you like to have them do together with you?

    b. Have you ever talked to them about this?

    c. Is there anything you can do to help them so they would have more time to spend with you?

    d. Talk about this as a family.

2. What do we learn about Jesus' attitude toward children in Matthew 19:13-15?

A Verse to Remember:

"A child left to himself brings shame to his mother" (Prov. 29:15).

49

When I Grow Up

I wonder what I'll be when I grow up.
> An Olympic swimmer? Or a gymnast?
> A doctor?
> Or an airline pilot?
> Or a radio announcer?

I hope it'll be something big and important.
But I don't want to have to go to school too much.
But if I have to, you'll help me with that, too, won't you?
Do you know what I'll be when I grow up, Lord?
Do you have a special plan for me?
Or do I get to choose?

Let's Talk

1. What do you want to be when you grow up?
2. Ask your mother and dad how they chose the work they are doing.
3. If they could choose over again, what would your parents do?
4. Ask Mom and Dad what they think you will be able to do well when you grow up.
5. How many people get to be champions?
6. What does it take to become a champion?
7. Have you ever thought about asking God to guide you?
    a. Why is it wise to pray about something like this?
    b. Why not take a few minutes and pray about this right now?

A Verse to Remember:

"Trust in the Lord with all your heart. . . . In all your ways acknowledge him, and he will make straight your paths" (Prov. 3:5, 6).

A note to parents:

If your child has a special interest in some vocation, invite someone who does that work to come for a meal. They can describe their work and tell what training is needed, etc.

50

I Hate Being Somebody's Brother

I hate it, Lord!
At school everybody says,
   "Oh, you're Jason Moore's brother,"
or,
   "You're Jennifer's little brother, aren't you?"
Why can't people let me be me?
Why do they think just because Jason's a good ball player,
   I should be?
I hate baseball!
Or why do they think just because Jennifer's good at math,
   I should be?
I hate math!
Why can't people just let me be me?

Let's Talk

1. Have you ever had people compare you with someone else
or expect you to do as well as someone else?

   a. How does that make you feel?

   b. Can Mother and Dad tell about an instance when this
happened to them?

   c. Even if people don't say anything, is there someone
Mom and Dad wish they were like instead of being themselves?

   d. How does this make them feel?

2. The ancient Hasidic (pious) Jews had a statement worth
thinking about: "Each man shall know and consider that in his

qualities he is unique in the world, and that none like him has ever lived before. For, had there ever been someone like him, then he would not have needed to exist."

3. Now read the above statement again and put in your own name instead of "each man" and "him." How does reading it that way make you feel?

4. Now read and discuss 1 Corinthians 12:14-26. Then go around your family circle and take turns sayir . One gift I see Dad has is—(for example, patience)." "One gift I see Mother has is—(for example, understanding)," etc. Do this for each family member.

5. Close with a prayer of thanks that God has made each of us unique individuals, and each one is valuable.

A Verse to Remember:

"Having gifts that differ according to the grace given to us, let us use them" (Rom. 12:6).

51

Why Do Parents Let You Win?

I played checkers with Dad last night, Lord,
    and I won.
I think he *let* me win.
Why do parents do that, Lord?

Let's Talk

1. Why do you think parents let you win when you play games with them?

2. How do you feel when you can ride a bike faster than Mom? How would you feel if she pedaled fast and rode away from you?

3. Do you have any friends whom you sometimes let win? How do you feel when you let them win?

4. Games and play are meant for more than winning. Games and play are meant for making and enjoying friends. Have fun when you play!

A Verse to Remember:

"Do nothing from selfishness or conceit, but in humility count others better than yourselves" (Phil. 2:3).

52

Praise the Lord!

Praise the Lord!
Oh, skateboard,
 I say,
  glide smoothly and swiftly,
  and praise the Lord!
Oh, all my train engines,
 I say,
  puff and chug
  and praise the Lord!
Oh, my skipping rope,
 I say,
  twirl and twirl
  and praise the Lord!
Oh, my five-speed bike,
 I say,
  go fast!
  and praise the Lord!
Oh, all my toys,
 I say,
  stand up
  and praise the Lord!

Let's Talk

1. An old song says, "You're not fully dressed until you wear a smile." Jesus wants to be with us in all the minutes of our day. When we realize He is with us, we will feel happy. How great it is when our hearts bubble over with so much love for Him that we want even our toys to praise Him.

2. When you feel really happy, how do you express your happiness?

3. Now it's your turn to write a psalm of praise. Mother and Dad should each write one, too.

4. After you have written your psalms, read them aloud to each other and praise the Lord together.

A Verse to Remember:

"Thou, O Lord, hast made me glad by thy work; at the works of thy hands I sing for joy" (Ps. 92:4).